A Sketch of Mota Grammar

A

SKETCH

OF

MOTA GRAMMAR.

BY

THE REV. R. H. CODRINGTON, M.A.,

FELLOW OF WADHAM COLLEGE, OXFORD.

LONDON:

PRINTED BY GILBERT AND RIVINGTON,

52, ST. JOHN'S SQUARE, CLERKENWELL.

1877.

A SKETCH OF MOTA GRAMMAR.

I. ALPHABET.

THE letters are used on the principle of representing the sound of the Mota by the letter which represents not the same, but the corresponding sound in English. The power of the letters in the two languages is very rarely identical, but in most cases the difference is slight. The following are the most important differences :—

1. *g* is in no case the same as in English, but represents a consonant common to all Melanesian tongues.

2. *q* represents a compound consonant in which *k p w* are present, with varying prominence in various words.

3. *n̈* represents the English *ng* in singer, not that in finger. Because the Mota *g* is not the English *g* the sound of *ng* in Mota (as in *tangae*, a tree) is altogether different to the English ng, in either of its two sounds. In writing, or in printing in italics, this sound is represented by *n̈*; in printing in ordinary type by an italic *n*.

The letters used are *a e g i k l m n o p q r s t u v w*.

Before *r*, after *n* and *l*, there is an euphonic sound of *d*; as *nan ra* sounds *nandra*; and *pul rua*, *puldrua*; but the *d* is not written, as the words are *nan* and *ra*, *pul* and *rua*, and it is only a way of pronouncing *r* to please the ear. *m* is often pronounced very broadly, as if *mw*.

The vowel sounds represented by *a e i o u* are perhaps ten; *a e i o* having a long or short sound, *u* only a long one, as English *oo*, and *o* a third, peculiar, approaching *u*.

The only true diphthongs are *ai, ae, ao, au*.

The proper vowel sounds are represented by the vowel letters, not the English sounds. *w* is commonly used to close a syllable; *u* at the end of a word often is very faintly pronounced.

(For notes on the Dialects more appropriate here see page 31.)

II. ARTICLES.

The Mota Articles are three—*o, na, i*.

1. 2. *O* is the more common, *na* being used only when the noun has a pronominal affix : *o ima*, ' a or the house ; ' *naimak*, ' my house.'

There is no distinction of definite and indefinite, but both articles are, as regards the mind of the native, probably definite.

There is no distinction of number : *o ima*, ' a house ; ' *o ima ñañ*, ' houses.'

3. *i* is a Personal Article, used with Personal Nouns, as *na* and *o* with common nouns ; *o* being used with names of places.

i is used with all names, native or foreign : *i Sarawia, i Palmer*. It is also used with the interrogative ' who ? ' *isei?* It has also the power, not only of showing a word to be the name of a person, not of a thing, but of personifying the notion conveyed by a noun or a verb.

This power of the personal article with a verb produces something resembling a participle : *gale*, ' to deceive ; ' *i gale*, ' the deceiver ; ' but this is only used when something like a title or special appellation is in view.

(*Caution.*—In the translation of St. John this is often wrong.)

This power of *i* with a noun is simple, conveying what

a capital letter does in English: *i Vat*, 'the Rock;' *i Vavae*, 'the Word;' *i Nun*, 'the True One.'

It is probably a consequence of native names having always a significance with them, that, whether inter-rogatively or demonstratively, the personal article used with the word for 'thing' means a person. Thus, *gene*, 'a thing;' *o gene iloke*, 'this thing;' *i gene iloke*, 'this person.' *O sava ?* 'what?' *I sava ?* 'who ?' The feminine is *iro*. *Ro* is prefixed to *native* female names, not to foreign ones, and can be used without *i* as well as with; but *i* is the article, *ro* not.

The presence of *ro* shows the word to have become a native feminine name; as in ordinary personal names, and, as above, in personification; and shows, in the same way, a female to be spoken of or inquired about: *iro gale*, 'the female deceiver;' *iro gene*, 'the woman;' *iro sava ?* 'what woman ?'

Ro is not used with foreign names, because they have no signification: *i Sara, i Mary, i Ono*. *I* and *iro* are used with names also of animals. The *plural* is *ira*, masculine; *ira ro*, feminine; but the *article* of these is *i*.

III. NOUNS.

Nouns Substantive, i. e. the names of things, are divided in Mota (as in Fiji), into two classes, viz., those that do and do not take the pronominal affix, with the article *na*. This division is almost exhaustive; there are but very few words with which, according to strict native usage, the two forms of the possessive can be used.

(*Caution.*—In our translations, till of late, errors are common.)

The principle of this division appears to be a nearer or more remote connection between the possessor or the possessed. Parts of a body, or of an organization, the ordinary equipment and properties of a man, things in which proprietorship seems most nearly involved—these take the pronominal affix. Other nouns, a more distant notion of relation to which exists, are incapable of this affix. This appears to be the principle; but the application of it in particular is in some cases unintelligible, e.g. 'a man's bag,' is *na taña na*; 'his basket,' *non o gete*; 'his bow' is *na us una*; 'his paddle,' *non o wose*.

This distinction is common to all Melanesian languages.

A second division of nouns is according to termination:—

1. Some have a termination marking a substantive in what may be called its nominative case, *i. e.* as it stands unaffected by connection with another word.

2. Others have no such termination.

These two classes of substantives again approach the division before mentioned, those (1) which have a special termination, being generally names of things which are relative to some other things; those (2) which have not, being generally the names of things which have an absolute existence of their own. It will consequently be mostly the case that nouns which can also be used as verbs belong to the first class; the names of things as such not bearing use as verbs.

Of the second class, nouns with no special termination, it is unnecessary to say anything.

The first class may be divided according to the termination affixed to the radical word :—

a. If the radical ends in a vowel, *i* is affixed, and sometimes *e*; e.g. *sasa-i*, 'a name;' *vava-e*, 'a word;' *tuqe-i* 'a garden;' *roro-i*, 'a report.'

b. If the radical ends in a consonant the termination *iu* or *ui* (according to dialect) is affixed; e.g. *tol-iu*, 'an egg;' *qat-ui*, 'head;' *qeteg-iu*, 'beginning.'

This termination, as above stated, is an addition to the radical word; and it drops when, in what corresponds to the inflection of a possessive case, the pronoun is affixed, thus *na-sasa-k*, 'my name;' *na-tuqe-ma*, 'your garden.' It also drops in composition with another word; as, *tol toa*, 'a fowl's egg;' *o qat qoe*, 'a pig's head.'

INFLECTION.

It will have been seen that there is something of inflection in what may be called the possessive case of the noun (though the word inflected represents the thing possessed, not the possessor) ; but this is indeed but the rejection of termination, and not the modification of the true noun : *i.e.* in *qat qoe*, ' a pig's head,' *qat* is the true form of the word, which is lengthened into *qatui*, when it stands absolute, by the special substantival termination *ui.*

There is besides a further and truer inflection undergone by words whose radical ends in the vowel *a*, which in what has been called the possessive case becomes *e.* Thus *sasaI*, ' a name,' standing absolute, and with the termination ; *na-sasa-k*, ' my name,' the radical with the pronominal affix ; but *o sasE tanun*, ' a man's name,' with the radical inflected in the possessive case.

It is, however, probably much better not to speak of a possessive case, but to regard the word as in composition, in which the first member of the compound very naturally takes a lighter termination.

But it should be observed that when the two substantives thus form a compound word, it represents what in English would be expressed by the possessive case. When in an adjective, *i. e.* where it qualifies the noun, there is no compound form, there is no inflection in Mota : thus *o ime qoe*, ' a pig's house,' with the notion of a pig whose house it is ; but *o ima qoe*, ' a pig house,' as distinct from a man's habitation. *O sinage vui*, ' a spirit's food ; ' *o sinaga vui*, ' spiritual food.'

(*Caution.*—There are some errors in this matter in our translations.)

This inflection obtains in words whose radicals end in *a*, whether they take a substantival termination or not. *Naui*, ' a leaf,' is inflected *no* ; *no tangae*, ' a tree's leaf,' an example of a small class. It is desirable perhaps here to show a noun with the pronominal affix ; thus—*napanek*, 'my hand;' *napanema*, 'your hand;' *napanena*, 'his hand;' *napanenina*, 'our hand,' inclusive; *napanemam*, 'our hand,' exclusive; *napanera*, 'their hand.'

Where the radical ends with a consonant the affix *k*, *ma*, *na*, &c., is assisted with a vowel, *i* or *u*, according to dialect: *nāqatuk* or *naqatik*, 'my head;' *naqetegina*, 'its beginning.'

A great number of words are indifferently used as verbs or substantives; but there is, as above mentioned, a common use of a termination marking a word as a noun. Besides this there is a form of verbal substantive, the verb with, generally, the termination *va*: *mule* 'to go;' *muleva*, 'a going;' *tape*, 'to love;' *tapeva*, 'love,' *i. e.* loving.

This verbal substantive is sometimes formed with *ga*: *vano* 'to go;' *vanoga*, 'a going.' Sometimes with *ra*: *toga* 'to stay;' *togara* 'staying,' way of life. Sometimes with *ia*: *nonom*, 'to think;' *nonomia*, 'thought, thinking.' Sometimes with *a*: *mate*, 'to die;' *matea*, 'death.'

Compound Nouns follow the last member as regards inflection: *natano-panek*, 'my handiwork;' *tanoi*, 'a place;' *panei*, 'a hand.' But *nok o tano-pul* 'my candlestick;' *tanoi*, 'a place;' *pul*, 'candle,' *panei* belonging to one class, *pul* to the other.

It may be observed that a noun only takes the pronominal affix when used in its primary sense; when it has a secondary use it cannot be so used. Thus *panei* is not only 'a hand' or 'arm,' but 'an armlet;' and it is not possible to say *napanek*, 'my armlet,' but *nok o panei*.

Number.—There is no mark of number in the noun; the addition of *ñañ* makes a plural.

IV. ADJECTIVES.

The qualification of a substantive is most commonly effected in Mota by a verb, not by an adjective, e. g. *o tanun we tatas*, ' a bad man '=a man (who) is bad. This is in fact the ordinary way of speaking, and the true adjectives in the language are few. There are, however, some words, that is to say, not substantives, which may be used adjectively to qualify, as above, *sinaga vui*, ' spirit (= spiritual) food ;' not words which are really verbs, used where in English an adjective would be used ; but words signifying a quality, and coming after the substantive to qualify the idea.

It is possible that all these true adjectives might be soon written down, but a few examples will suffice :— *O ima mantagai*, ' a small house ;' *o ima liwoa*, ' a large house.' *Mantagai* and *liwoa* have no use as substantives ; they are here adjectives purely. These, and indeed all adjectives can be used as verbs, *o ima* WE *mantagai, o ima* WE *liwoa*, but with a slight corresponding change of sense.

Degrees of comparison are expressed by prepositions and adverbs :—' A horse is bigger than a cow,' *O horse we poa* NAN *o kau*—is big away from. ' We are more than they,' *Kamam we qoqo* SAL *neira*—many over and above them. ' This is the biggest,' *iloke we poa aneane*— big exceedingly. It is sufficient to express comparison to say merely, ' This is big.' *Iloke we poa*, it being understood that a comparison is made in the mind.

V. NUMERALS.

Numerals are in use, sometimes substantives, sometimes adjectives, and sometimes are used in the form of verbs.

1. The *cardinals* are (1) *tuwale*, (2) *nirua*, (3) *nitol*,

(4) *nivat*, (5) *tavelima*, (6) *laveatea*, (7) *lavearua*, (8) *laveatol*, (9) *laveavat*, (10) *sañavul*. There are evidently two sets of five : *rua, tol, vat,* being 2, 3 and 4, on the first hand, with *ni* prefixed ; on the second hand, with *lavea*.

Ni is a verbal form, sometimes prefixed also to *tuwale*. The verbal particles (hereafter to be mentioned) are freely applied to all the cardinals, taking the place of *ni* in 2, 3 and 4. All the cardinals, used as *adjectives*, come after the noun : One man, *O tanun tuwale ;* Ten men, *o tanun sañavul. Sañavul,* ten, used as a *substantive*, comes first, followed by other cardinals used as *adjectives : sañavul tol,* 'tens three' = 30. *Sañavul,* 'ten,' *melnol,* '100,' *tar,* '1000,' as *substantives* take, the two latter require, multiplicatives : *sañavul vagatol,* 'ten three times' = 30 ; *melnol vagavat,* 'hundred four times' = 400 ; *tar vagatuwale,* 'thousand once' = 1000. But it may be *sañavul tol.*

2. *Multiplicatives* are the cardinals with *vaga* or *va* prefixed : *vagavatuwale,* ' once ;' *vagavatalima,* ' five times.'

3. *Ordinals* are formed from cardinals by the addition of various terminations, with, in the case of 2, 3 and 4, the prefix *vaga* or *va :*—2nd, 3rd and 4th, *vagaruei* or *varuei, vaga* or *va-toliu, vaga* or *va*VATIU ; 5th, 6th and 7th, *tavelima*I, *lavetea*I, *laverua*I ; 8th, 9th and 10th, *lavetoli*U, *lavevati*U, *sañavuli*U ; 100th, *melnol*ANAE. There is no ordinal to the cardinal *tuwale ; moai* is ' first.'

Obs. :—Ni, not properly part of the ordinal, is dropped from 2nd, 3rd and 4th ; and *a* from *lavea* in 6th, 7th 8th and 9th.

4. *Numeration* in Mota is clear, if lengthy. There is a word to express the units above tens, the substantive *o numei ;* and another to express units or tens above hundreds, *o avaviu.* 1876 is thus expressed : *tar vatuwale, melnol vagalaveatol, o avaviu sañavul lavearua* (or *vagalavearua*), *o numei laveatea ; i. e.* thousand once,

hundreds eight times, the sum above the hundreds seven tens (or seven times ten), the sum above the tens six. Other shorter examples : Eleven, *sañavul tuwale o numeī tuwale ; i. e.* ten, one, the unit above, one. Thirty, *sañavul tol*, tens three. Thirty-three: *sañavul tol o numei nitol ;* 106, *melnol vatuwale o avaviu laveatea ; i. e.* hundred once, the sum above, six.

VI. PRONOUNS.

1. *Personal Pronouns.*

Singular :	1.	*Inau, nau, na.*
	2.	*Iniko, ko, ka.*
	3.	*Ineia neia, ia, a, ni.*
Dual :	1.	{ *Ikara, kara,* exclusive. { *Inara, nara,* inclusive.
	2.	*Ikamurua, kamurua, kamrua.*
	3.	*Irarua, rarua, irara, rara.*
Trial :	1.	{ *Ikatol, katol,* exclusive. { *Inatol, natol,* inclusive.
	2.	*Ikamtol, kamtol.*
	3.	*Iratol, ratol.*
Plural :	1.	{ *Ikamam, kamam,* exclusive. { *Inina, nina,* inclusive.
	2.	*Ikamiu, kamiu, kam.*
	3.	*Ineira, neira, ira, ra.*

The personal article *i* in these Pronouns is used or disused at pleasure.

The exclusive and inclusive forms of the first person are used when the speaker excludes or includes the person or persons to whom he is speaking ; ' You and I,' is *nara,* ' He and I ' is *kara.*

1. The short form *na* in the first person is used only before, never after a verb. It is used indifferently, with *nau*, in direct indicative sentences, but is alone correct in

subjoined construction. *Nau me ilo* or *na me ilo*, ' I saw ; ' but *Nau we mule si* NA *ilo*, ' I am going, that I may see.'

2. *Ka* in the second person is also used only in subjoined clauses, and in the imperative. *Ko* becomes *iko* when affixed after a consonant, in which use *i* is not the personal article but euphonic.

3. *Ineia, neia, ni* in direct construction ; *ni* only in subjoined and imperative. *Ia, a,* are used only in the objective, and, affixed to the verb or preposition : *Na me sike*A, *me tataga suri*A, ' I sought him and looked after him.'

4. In the second person plural, *kam* can only be used as the subject.

5. In the third person *ira* and *ra* as *ia* and *a* in the singular. *Ira* and *ra*, when subjects in a sentence, are the article.

The *pronominal affixes*, giving a possessive sense with nouns, are no doubt only pronouns, in the form *k, ma, na,* &c. It is equally right, but not so idiomatic, to add the pronouns in the ordinary form, to say *ima inau*, instead of *imak*. In other Melanesian tongues, the pronouns in the form *k, ma, na*, substantially, but variously modified, are used as affixes to verbs and prepositions. In Mota there is one remnant, or representative, of this use in the word *apena*, ' in reference to it, about it '—the preposition *ape* with *na*.

The analogy of other languages makes it very probable that the *n*, which occurs in the so-called possessive case when persons are referred to, is this pronoun *na*. Thus, *natanopane*N*sei iloke ? natanopane*N *Wogale*, ' Whose handwriting is this ? Wogali's.' This is restricted to animate objects ; thus, *ni we pute ape kiki*N *o tanun*, ' he sits by the man's side ; ' but *ape kiki ima*, ' by the side of the house.' *Ni we pute vawo kula*N *o horse*, ' he sits on the back of the horse ; ' but *ni we pute ape kule* *ima*, ' he sits at the back of the house.' When the pronominal affix begins with *r*, *n* is added at the end of the substantive, but not always ; thus, ' the house of two,' *imanrara* or *imarara*. It is possible that this is the pronoun *na* ; it occurs commonly after certain prepositions.

INTERROGATIVE PRONOUNS.

For persons, *sei* is used ; for things, *sava*, ' what ? '

Sei takes the personal article, *isei ? irosei ? irasei ? irarosei ?* perhaps always when the subject, but very commonly not after a verb or preposition. *Sei* is no doubt a substantive ; *sava* is a noun substantive in all respects.

RELATIVE PRONOUNS.

There are no relative pronouns as such ; when a relative would be used in English, the sense is conveyed in Mota :—

1. By the personal pronoun : *I gene me gaganag, ko me vatran*IA *ma ti*, ' The man whom you sent told me,' *i.e.* ' The man told, you sent him here.'

2. By adding a verb without a conjunction : *I gene me ilo me gaganag*, ' The man (who) saw it told me,' or *I gene me gaganag me ilo*, ' the man told (who) saw.'

3. By the word used as the interrogative pronoun : *Ni me gaganag mun*RASEI, *me vatatua*, ' He told those who met him.' This corresponds to ' whoever,' rather than ' who.'

DEMONSTRATIVE PRONOUNS.

These are—*iloke*, ' this ; ' *iloke ñañ*, ' these ; ' *ilone*, ' that ; ' *ilone ñañ*, ' those ; ' *o ike*, ' this ; ' *o ike ñañ*, ' these ; ' *o ine*, ' that ; ' *o ine ñañ*, ' those.'

Ke and *ne* are particles of place. The difference is remarkable that the article cannot be used with *iloke, ne ;* but always is used with *ike, ine*. The personal article is used with *ike, ne; i ike,* 'this fellow;' *iro ine,* 'that woman.'

POSSESSIVE PRONOUNS.

It is evident that the work of possessive pronouns is done for one large division of Mota words by the affixed personal pronouns; but there remains the other division, the class of words to which the pronominal affix does not apply. With them, however, the same usage really prevails, though in the use of words which have the appearance of personal pronouns. These are—*nok,* 'my;' *noma,* 'thy;' *nona,* 'his;' *nonara* inclusive, *nonkara* exclusive, 'belonging to us two;' *nomurua,* 'belonging to you two;' *nomam* exclusive, *nonina* inclusive, 'our;' *nomiu,* 'your;' *nora,* 'their.' There is equally common the form *anok, anoma,* &c. *Amok mok, amoma,* &c., is also my, thy, &c., with a slightly closer relation implied, as of origination.

Anak, anama, &c., in no case *nak, nama,* is used with regard to persons: *o rowrowovag anak,* 'my servant.'

It is evident upon the face of it that there is here only a substantive with the pronominal affix. This becomes more distinct on observing the form *nanok, namok,* with the article; and also the words used as possessive pronouns in regard to things eaten, or drunk, and possessions regarded as choice properties.

A thing for my eating is *gak,* your *gama,* and so on.

    „   „   drinking is *mak,* your *mama,* &c.

'A pig,' 'a fruit tree,' is *pulak, pulama,* &c.

These words then apply as apparent personal pronouns to the class of Mota nouns which do not take the pronominal affix. Thus, *nok o gasal,* 'my knife;' *moma* or *mom o vavae,* 'your word;' *nona* or *non o togara,* 'his behaviour;' and so on throughout the persons.

If *anok, amok,* is used, it generally follows the noun, *nok* and *mok* never do: *o gasal anok, o vavae amoma.*

Mok, amok, namok, are used in the sense of "my

doing " in such a way as to represent something like a passive participle. "The word spoken by the Prophet," *o vavae amon o Prophet me vava*, i. e. "The word, it was the Prophets doing (that) spoke it." At the end of a book, "Printed by A. Lobu, H. Silter, and others," "*Namora A. Lobu, H. Silter*, &c., *me qisañ*," "The doing of A. L., H. S., &c. (who) printed it."

Nok and *mok* are used very indifferently, and yet *mok* is more correct where a thing is not regarded as a mere possession, but in a sense a product *Mok o vavae* is more natural for 'my word,' and *nok o gasal* for 'my knife.'

VII. PREPOSITIONS.

The simple Prepositions in Mota are nine—*a, i, ape, mun, sur, nan, goro, nia, ama.*

Some of these, compounded or constructed with adverbs and nouns, form many prepositions in ordinary use whose force depends on the simple preposition in them. There is another, *ta*, which can hardly be counted with these.

1. *A* is a preposition of simple *local* force, "at." The Mota idiom is to say "at" when we should say "from." Thus, "I saw the ship from the cliff," *na me ilo o aka a mate nua*—I saw the ship *at* the cliff, *i.e.*, I was there when I saw the ship; "that came from Mota," *O gene me mule ma a Mota*—came hither at Mota, the locality of its coming.

2. *I* a preposition of *motion to*. This is of motion completed. *Ni me mule i taun*, "He has gone to town and has arrived."

3. *Ape* gives the sense of place with relation to something else, by, alongside of, against; and thence in reference, or regard to, concerning, because of. *Ipe* with the sense of motion is used, but very rarely. "He is standing by the fence," *Ni we tira ape geara.* "The plank leans against the house," *O irav we pesinag ape-*

ima.—" What for ? Why ?" *Ape sava, i. e.* in reference to what ?—" What about ? " *Ape sava, i. e.* concerning what ?—" I ran because of the rain," *na me valago ape wena.*

4. *Mun* conveys the notion of *transition*, as by an instrument or through a medium, or with the end attained. Hence *mun* may be translated commonly as 'by,' or 'through,' or 'with,' or 'to,' or 'for.' " He hit him with a stick,' *Ni me vusia mun o qat kere.*—" He got it by deceit," *Ni me taur mona mun o galeva.*—" Give it to me," *Le ma mun nau.*

" Through " at the end of prayers is rendered *mun.* " Who are you doing that for ? For myself." *Ko we ge munsei ? Mun nau kel.*

Mun is used in a peculiar manner to express the object of an action where we should use " for " or " as," and when nothing corresponding would be used in English : " He bought it for his own," *Ni me wol mun pulana.*—" He took him as his servant," *Ni me lavia mun rowrowovag anana.*—" I will be to him a father, and he shall be to me a son," *Na te munia mun tamana, wa ni te munau mun natuk.* In this use *mun* takes no article after it.

5. *Sur,* of *motion to a person,* never to a place of approach, not merely dative : " Go to him," *Mule suria.*"— " Give it to him," *Le munia,* not *sur.* This does not mean that *sur* is only used of personal approach, but that the notion is of bringing a thing closely home to a person if not of coming. Thus, *Ni me gaganag ma munau,* " He gave me information of it," merely dative ; but *Ni me gaganag ma sur nau* would imply that he brought the information ; and it might also be said that *Ni me gaganag ma sur nau mun o letas,* " by a letter."

6. *Nan* is simply " from " : " Where does this come from ? From Mota."—*Iloke we raule ma avea ? nan o Mota ma. Nan* is used at the end of a sentence without a

substantive after it, referring back to a substantive that has gone before. "That is his own place that he has gone away from."—*Ilone navanuana ni me toa veta nan.*

7. *Goro* is the most difficult of the prepositions. There is always the notion of motion in it, and of motion over against. If a rail simply stands against a fence with nothing against which it bears up, the preposition is *ape*, but if it stands as a prop, it would be *goro*. If a man stands before another, with no reference to motion; he stands *ape nagona;* but if he has come to stand, *goro nanagona*, not at his face, but against his face.

With this is connected the sense of round about, as if surrounding for protection, or for a guard, as to fence round a garden: *geara goro o tuqei,* "To fence against pigs," *geara goro o qoe.* So a glass is round about a lamp, *waliog goro o pul.*

In very many cases *goro* will be translated "over," but always with the notion of motion and of action, not of mere superposition. To put on clothes is *saru goro natarapema mun o siopa*, to clothe over your body with a garment ; and the garment, *te toga goro natarapema*, covers over your body, as protection, or concealment, or decoration. In the same way to paint over a surface is to *lamas goro*. If anything be hung over the fire, with an express view to some action on or from the fire, the preposition will be *goro;* if with no such view, *avune.* If a person sits over the fire to look after it, *ni te pute goro av;* if he sits over it to get warmth from it, *te masil goro av.*

Then follows the further sense of "after" as applied to that which is the object of action. Thus, to look after, to take care of, is *ilo-goro;* to go after a thing, to fetch it, is *mule-goro.*

8. *Nia* is peculiar in its use, inasmuch as it never comes before, but always follows the noun to which it is applied: "This is the pen I wrote the letter with," *Iloke*

B

o qat raverave na me rave o letas ti nia, corresponding exactly to the English. This position is invariable ; and it also occurs after the verb *ris*, to turn, to change :'' the water that turned into wine, *o pei me ris wine nia;* in this corresponding to the English withal. That it is a preposition seems clear from its use in another language ; but from its use then, it may be said that *ni* is the preposition, and *a* the pronoun.

9. *Ama*, in its other form *amen*, is "with," in the sense of together with : "He lives with me," *Ni we toga amenau ;—amaiko*, 'with you.' It is very questionable, however, whether the preposition in this is not merely *a*, and the latter syllable a fragment of a noun. The form of it seems to indicate this : *am*EN *nau, am*ᴀ*iko, am*ᴀ*ia, am*EN *kamam, am*EN *nina, am*EN *kamiu, am*ᴀɪ*ra* or *am*EN*ra* or *am*E*ra*. The same may be said of *ape*, and the rare *ipe*.

Another simple preposition, if it can so be called, is *ta*, which is used in the sense of "of" when spoken of belonging to a place : A man of Mota, *o tanun ta Mota;* the language of Mota, *o vava ta Mota;* A Mota plant, *o tangae ta Mota;* You speak Mota, *ko we vava ta Mota;* A Mota person, *o ta Mota*. This is probably in fact a substantive, not in origin merely, but in native use.

Compound prepositions, have their force as such from the presence in them of one of the simple prepositions, and much most commonly of *a* and *i*.

1. *Alo*, 'in,' *ilo*, 'into,' compounded of *a* and *i*, with a noun which with the reduplication is *loloi*, 'inside;' *sa alele*, *ilele*, 'inside ;' *avune*, 'above,' 'on ;' *ivune*, 'above,' 'on to ;' *vunai*, 'the upper side ;' *alalañe*, 'under ;' *ilalañe*, 'under,' with sense of motion; *lalañai*, 'under side;' *apan*, 'beside ;' *panei*, 'a hand;' *a tavala*,' 'beyond ;' *tavaliu*, 'side.'

2. With *alo* and *ilo*, *alovatitnai, ilovatitnai*, between.

3. An adverb with *nan*, 'out from ;' *lue nan*, 'down

from ;' *siwo nan,* ' up from ;' *kalo nan,* where we should say ' off.'

4. Adverb with *goro* where we should say ' across,' ' against,' ' about ;' *wolowolo goro, tatu goro* (meeting), *waliog goro.*

5. Add to these, *Complex Prepositions* as they may be called, because though no part is a preposition the whole word has the use and form of one, as *raveaglue,* ' through.'

6. Also words in other use adverbs and verbs, as the case may be, but serving as prepositions : *leas,* ' instead of ;' *tataga,* ' according to ;' *peten,* ' close to.'

In both compound and complex prepositions one of the members of the composition has the transitive force, whether a preposition as *alalane,* or an adverb as *waliog,* and the two parts are grammatically distinct. It is as reasonable and convenient, however, to write and treat them as one word, as the English words ' around,' ' among,' &c.

It should be remarked that whereas when a *thing* is spoken of, some of these compound prepositions, as *avune, alalane,* may be called prepositions, as ' above,' ' below,' in English; yet when a person is spoken of, the compound word cannot be taken for a preposition, but its composition from a preposition and a substantive is too conspicuous to be mistaken. For example : It fell on a stone, *me masu avune vat ;* but, A stone fell on me, *o vat me masu avunak.* In both cases *a* is the preposition, and *vune* or *vunak* an inflected *vunai ;* but one may call *avune* a preposition, but could not possibly think *avunak, avunama, avunana* such.

VIII. ADVERBS.

There is little to be said of these parts of speech, which in most cases are naturally only verbs or nouns, substantive or adjective, used adverbially, and in Mota without any modification of form. It naturally also is the case that many adverbs have no visible connection with other forms, whatever their real origin may be. These latter are probably the adverbs of place and time rather than of manner. The foremost of these in conspicuous use are *ma* and *at*, conveying the idea of 'hitherward' and 'outward,' used continually to indicate direction of motion or of thought: thus, 'give,' *le ma, le at*, according as the giving is to be to or away from the speaker;—something that has always been here, *me toga ran ma iake*.

Place and *time* are generally conceived as the same; but there are special adverbs of time, as *añaisa*, 'hereafter;' *anañaisa*, 'heretofore;' *añaisa?* 'when?' *anañaisa?* 'when?' in past time; '*qarig* or *a qarig*, 'to-day,' in present or future time; *anaqarig*, 'to-day,' in past; *ananora*, 'yesterday,' also *nanora; arisa*, 'the day after to-morrow;' *anarisa*, 'the day before yesterday.' In these there is evidently the local preposition *a* with a substantive. This is equally plain in *avea, ivea*, where, whither.

The particles *ne* and *ke* convey the idea in place or time of 'there,' and 'here,' and appear in the pronouns *ike, ine, iloke, ilone*, and these are adverbial particles: *ilokenake*, 'now;' *iake*, 'here;' *iane*, 'there;'* — *nake* and *nane* being used to give definiteness of thought as well as of position.

The adverbs 'above,' 'below,' &c. are expressed by *avunana, alalañana, i.e.* above it, below it, impersonally.

Adverbs of Number are the multiplicatives already mentioned—'once,' 'twice,' *vaga* or *va-tuwale, vagarua*, &c.

The notion of *place* occurs in one instance at least where *manner* is signified, in asking how? *tama avea?*

---

* *ia* is itself an adverb, though never occurring alone—*aia = a*, 'at,' and *ia:* The other world, *o maramu iloneia;* that is *ilone*, 'that;' *ia*, 'there.'

'like where,' instead of 'like what,' which, however, is also in use—*tam o sava?*

If the *affirmative* and *negative* are to be considered in this place, ' Yes ' is expressed in words by *we nun*, a verb, 'true ;' but also by exclamation and gesture. ' No,' is *tagai*, a substantive ; ' not ' is *gate* in the present and past, *tete* in the future.

IX. CONJUNCTIONS.

The Conjunction used for ordinary connection is *wa*, which is simply equivalent to " and."

Nan is a connective in narration, without any logical force. It may begin a narration, like " now " in English. *Adversative* Conjunctions are *pa, nava, panava*, each more strongly adversative than the other. *Pa*, is weak, and in very common use is separate only by a shade of meaning from *wa*. *Nava* is decided by ' but.' *Panava*, composed of the two others equals, ' notwithstanding.'

' If ' is *si ;* ' As ' is *tama*. Prepositions and adverbs supply the place of other conjunctions.

When words are quoted, *wa* is always used before the quotation ; and, often besides, *si* in the sense of ' that.' Thus, He said that he was coming, *Ni me vet wa si ni we mule ma ;* or it may be, He said I am coming, *Nan neia wa, Na we mule at*. If the words are directly or indirectly quoted, *wa* must be used ; but if the quotation is direct there is no need of *si*.

When the conjunction " and " is used in English, there is commonly used in Mota a form which is not a conjunction, but requires notice in this place. Thus, I and my brother, *tak tasik ;* Peter and John, Peter *tana* John ; You and who besides ? *Tama isei mulan* —and so on, *tamam, tamiu, tara*, &c.

This is evidently a substantive equivalent to fellow or companion, " my companion, my brother :" Peter went up, his companion John. *Tak* is a common appellative, like "mate."

This use is confined to persons, and to things which can naturally be regarded as going together, as fellows.

X. VERBS.

A Verb in Mota is a word used in a verbal form. There are indeed some words whose natural use is in a verbal form, some which having a special verbal termination are particularly verbs; but any word with which the verbal particles are used is so far forth a verb, whether substantive or adjective, or preposition, or adverb, or even article perhaps, in its more proper use.

Thus, *Me qoñ veta*, "It is already night;"— *qoñ* is a substantive. *O ima me mantagai munina*, "the house has become too small for us;" *mantagai* is an adjective. *Ni me siwo ma*, "He came down hither;"— *siwo* is an adverb. *Nau te munia mum tamana*, "I will be to him a father;"— *mun*, a preposition. *O matava wa o ravrav me o qoñ vagaruei*, "The morning and the evening were the second day;"— *o* is the article, but perhaps here it is the clause *o qoñ vagaruei*, which has become a verb.

On the other hand, words like *nonom*, 'think,' *sua*, 'paddle,' representing operations of the mind and body, are true verbs, and have to undergo an alteration to become substantives—*nonomia, suava*.

The prefixing or affixing of a syllable or letter of a certain character will make a verb with a special force out of a verb, or out of a word which may have been before either verb or substantive. Thus, *esu*, 'live' or 'life,' and *vaeseu*, 'make to live;' *roño*, to be in a state as patient not agent, and *roñotag*, to hear or feel.

Before the consideration of special forms of verbs, comes that of the verbal particles which are the signs of a verb, and in which in so many cases the verbal force seems to reside.

The Verbal Particles.

It should be noted that this is a common characteristic of all Melanesian tongues to mark tense and mood; in some others, but not in Mota, number and person, by particles coming before the Verb. In nothing is the variable character of the Melanesian speech more conspicuous than in the variation in the several dialects of these particles, with the universal employment of them.

In Mota these particles are *we, me, te, qe, ta, ti*, and they undergo no change to signify number or person. The use of *ti* is double, as it comes before or after the verb.

The Particles may be divided into *temporal* and *modal*. The *temporal* are *we, me, te, ti;* the *modal* are *qe, ta, ti*.

Temporal Particles.

The *present* is signified by *we*, the *past* by *me*, the *future* by *te*. This is not to be understood as if the time fixed by these particles is always the same as that which tenses in English would convey ; but what is of the present time, or of the past, or of the future, as it comes before the speaker's mind is represented in speech accordingly by these particles.

We.—If I say, *Nau we pute we raverave*, "I am sitting writing," the particle *we* conveys completely the present time. If, in a narrative, I say that some one came in and saw me sitting and writing, *Wa si sei me mule pata ma me ilo inau we pute we raverave*, the particle *me* conveys the sense of past time in the person's coming in; but *we* conveys the notion that what I was doing was present at the time spoken of. In this way a verb with *we* in Mota commonly stands in place of an adjective. Again, if two verbs are closely connected in a phrase which conveys something of a compound action, and not two successive stages in the action, if *me* or *te* mark the time as past or future for the first verb, the

second will have *we*. Thus, "The Apostles bore witness," *Ira Sala me gaganag we tira;* "Ye shall bear
witness," *Kamiu te gaganag we tira.*

When, however, successive actions are recounted, it is
not enough to fix the time to be past or future at the
beginning, and to go on with *we*, as if a particle con-
junctive merely of one verb to another, and devoid of the
sense of time. To relate the past in the present tense is
common enough.

Me.—If I write that "I was sitting and writing," *Si
na me pute pute we raverave,* the time is clearly marked
by *me* as past; and, as before mentioned, in a narrative
related as in the past, *me* will recur in each stage of the
narration. But *me* is used when the mind of the speaker
is looking back upon something, which perhaps has not
occurred in fact, but is presupposed in view of its conse-
quences: "If I were to do so I should die," *Si na me
ge tamaine, na me mate.* So very often *me* is used with
regard to the future, and in a strongly future sense;
what is still in fact future being viewed as so certain, as to
be spoken of as past. A boy asking leave to go and fish
on a night when leave is given will say, *Na me mule ilau,*
"I have gone to the beach," *i. e.* am going. To convey
a strong notion of the past, *me* is hardly enough; but
the complete perfect is shown by *veta*, 'already,' *Ni me
mate veta,* "He is dead."

Te is the sign of the future, and distinctly conveys a
future sense. It is common, however, to add *añaisa*,
'hereafter,' to mark a distinctly future meaning. *Te* is
used to signify what is habitual in action, and can be regarded as certain to be done, in the way in which 'will'
is used in English.

Ti.—The use of *ti*, in a temporal sense, is double, as it
comes before or after the verb.

1. *Before the verb* it has the sense of immediate suc-
cession of one action upon another; or else of constant
invariable action or condition. The notion of continu-

ance is common to both uses. In a narrative, when the words of the person whose acts are narrated are given, it is most common to use *ti*, because of the speaking being in a manner part of the action, not a subsequent occurrence. In the same way, when a person goes and does something for which he goes, and in all cases of the kind; so that *ti* comes to be very much of a narrative particle, and divested to a great extent of the character of time. Invariable condition is expressed by *ti*, as of a house in regard to its position, *ti taqa a pan matesala,* stands beside the road ;—A flower or fruit of its season, *O gaviga ti tawaga alo rara,* flowers in the winter: or its habit, *O no paka ti nun saru, ti awisaga gaplot kel,* A banian sheds its leaves and soon buds again.

2. *After the verb,* in its temporal use, *ti* throws the time a step farther back, makes a pluperfect of a perfect : " He has brought back the book he has been reading," *Ni me la kel ma o book ni me vasvasago ti alolona.* It is not that in English the pluperfect is always used where *ti* is thus used in Mota; but that the Mota sentence can probably be always translated with the English pluperfect to give the full sense.

The other *modal* use of *ti* is quite distinct from this; as is also another, in which after a verb or substantive it has the sense of still remaining, or yet: *Mantagai ti,* " There is still a little."

Modal Particles.

Qe.—This particle has no regard to time, but may very well be regarded as marking something like a subjunctive mood: " If I should see him I will tell him," *Si na qe iloa na te gaganag munia apena.*—" I will do so if it be possible," *Na te ge mok sin qe lai.* The use is most common with *si*, ' if,' but *qe* is used without it: *Qe le we qoqo munsei te sike kel we qoqo nania,* " Be much given to a man, much shall be required of him again."

Ta is hardly distinguishable in sense from *qe*, but may

be thought perhaps to be more potential and optative than subjunctive. It is less frequently used with *si*, 'if,' *Na ta iloa na te vava*, "Supposing that I should see him, I will tell him." Or, *Si na ta iloa*, "If I should see him." When *ta* is used *te* will rather follow, when *qe* is used *te* or *we*: *Si na qe maros na we ge*, "If I like I do;" but *Si na ta maros na te ge*, "I shall if I like."

Ti, in what may be called its modal use, inasmuch as it has no reference to time, but indicates rather the manner of the action, follows the verb. Its sense is rather to moderate the force of the verb, in the way of mitigation or diminution. It is difficult in all cases to separate this use of *ti* from that in which it modifies time, or expresses the notion of something still remaining, but it is a distinct use. No word in English can translate it, but the word "just" gives a good deal of its meaning: *Le ma ti*, "Give it here, just give it here."

The Verb is used without any verbal particles:

1. In what may be called the *Infinitive* mood, in which it is in fact a substantive with a preposition or an article. Thus, "You came here to work," *kamiu me mule ma si a maumawui.—Te rusagia ape non o maumawui*, "He will be paid for his work."

2. In the *Imperative: Ka mule ka gaganag*, "Go and tell;" *Ni mule*, "Let him go;" *Neira mule, Nina mule*, "Let them, Let us go." The plural second person imperative is with *tur*, the dual second person *ura*, the trial *tol*. Thus, *tur mule*, "Go;" *Ura mule*, "You two go;" *Tol mule*, "You three."

3. *In a subjoined clause:* "I ordered him to go," *Na me vareg ti munia si ni mule*, "That he should go."—"I said that I would go," *Na me vet si na mule*.

4. In a *negative* sentence: "I don't wish," *Na gate maros.*—"I did not wish," *Na gate maros.*—"I shall not like it," *Na tete maros ran. Except* when *qe* and *te* are

used, *Sin qe tete maros, Ni ta tete maros*, "Should he not be willing."

III. Verbs with special Verbal Forms.

These forms consist of either a prefix or affix to a word, which then can be used in no other than a verbal sense, e.g. *esu*, 'live' or 'life,' but *vaesu*, 'to save or heal;' *mana*, 'to influence or influence,' but *manag*, 'to enable.'

There are many words, as before said, which are verbs only, but without a special form as such. These also take, some of them, a special form with a change of sense: *vava*, 'to speak,' *vavag*, to speak against a person.

Prefixes.

These are *va* and *ma*.

1. *Va.*—This is the form in Mota of a particle common to the Pacific languages, having the sense of 'make,' *vaesu*, 'to make live.' It is not used in the sense of originating anything, but of changing condition or character. This causative prefix is not in so frequent use in Mota as might be expected, the word for 'make,' *qe* or *na*, being very frequently used. It might be applied, however, to very many verbs and be intelligible.

2. *Ma* prefixed to an adverb makes a neuter verb; prefixed to a verb it makes a verb expressing condition. It is therefore a particle of condition, not of action; and a verb with *ma* has much of the sense of an adjective. It also answers to some extent the purpose of a passive. *Wora* is 'apart,' 'asunder,' *mawora* is 'parted,' 'sundered,' 'burst,' in a condition in which the thing is in parts. So *malate*, 'broken;' *manoanoa*, 'in fragments;' *magesei*, 'alone.' *Lakalaka* is 'to rejoice;' *malakalaka*, 'to be in a joyful state.' *Masekeseke*, 'light-hearted.' It is by no means meant that *ma* when the first syllable

of a word is in all cases this prefix, but that there is a prefix to verbs having this force.

Affixes.

These are very numerous, consisting either of a single consonant or a syllable; and the general force of all is transitive, to make every verb to which they are applied definitely transitive in sense, though very often there may be no expressed object in the sentence.

Roño is to be in a state of feeling or mind, a word never used by itself; but as *roño vivtig*, to be in pain; *roño gavir*, to suffer without complaint; *roño maul*, to be enduring; *ronotag* is to hear or to feel. *Vava*, to speak; but *vavag*, to speak against some one;—*vano*, to go; *vanogag*, to go with some thing to convey.

This does not apply only to verbs which are neuter before the affix is made, but to active verbs also, the various affixes defining the transitive force in one direction or another; thus, *koko* is to cover over with the hand, as the face, or something to be protected; it requires *goro* before the object. *Kokomag* is to be careful about; *Kokor*, to keep, as a rule or a covenant is kept; *kokos*, as a net incloses fish. Nor does this apply only to words which without it are in use as verbs, though much most commonly. *Matai*, 'an eye:' the verb 'to eye' is *matag*.

These affixes cannot be assigned each of them its own force; there is indeed only one which differs from the rest in this as signifying "with," as much as if it were a preposition, and in being separable; and this affix *vag* is better considered by itself, particularly as *vag* also is applied in the same way as all the other affixes, and is then like the other inseparable. It may be said then that the particular force of the affix in each case can only be learnt by the consideration of each case as it occurs; the general force being that given above. The natives themselves do not recognise any special force in any particular affix, always excepting *vag* when it is separable.

It will be convenient to divide these affixes into those which consist (1) of a letter, (2) of a syllable :—

1. The most common form is with *g*, as already given— *manag, matag, vavavag.* The other consonants employed are in much less frequent use :

n, as *sogon*, to stow away ; *v* as *sogov* to give freely, *sogo*, being to set out, as food ; *vanov*, put ; *vano*, go.

r, as *kokor ; vesager*, to place above, to put on the fire or the table ; *va, sage, r, sage*, up.

t, as *wonot*, to oppress ; *wono*, close ; *mavat*, to weigh upon ; *mava*, heavy.

s, as *kokos*.

The affix when a syllable is either *ag, gag, lag, mag, rag, sag, tag, vag*, without any difference in sense, but with regard perhaps to euphony : *Taleag*, turn ; *tale*, about ; *vanogag*, to conduct ; *vano*, to go ;—*saromag*, to sheath a knife ; *saro* to come in, as fish into a net ;—*vilerag*, to distribute ; *vile*, to take or bring ;—*porosag*, to mock ; *poro*, to mock ;—*roñotag*, as above ;—*sirvag*, to cut close, as grass ; *sir*, to shave.

The separable affix *vag* is not the same as this last, but is equivalent to a preposition : *mulevag*, to go with a thing ;—*matevag o gopae tutusag*, die with a fever ; *masvag o tapera*, fall down with a plate. This *vag* can go as a preposition, not with the verb but separated from it, and with the substantive : *mule raveaglue o tinesara vag o tapera*, go through the courtyard with a basket.

The Adverbs *reag* and *vitag* are affixed to verbs, but are not affixes of the character here spoken of : *mapreag*, put a thing away ; *nomvitag*, forgive, think off from.

Ga.—This is not an affix, but it is a termination very

common with verbs which do the work of adjectives, and which denote quality; it is often also *iga*. In the great number of instances in which it occurs it is not possible to find the word without the termination; as *aqaga*, 'white;' *turturuga*, 'blue.' In many others the root is found in another combination; as *ronoga*, famous, on account of wealth; *ronronotar*, multitude of possessions. In some the termination is added to a word in common use; as, *mamasa*, dry; *mamasaiga*, parched.

Reciprocal Verbs.

Reciprocity is denoted by the prefix *var*, very neatly and effectively: *Rara we varvava*, They two are conversing, reciprocally speaking; *Neira we varvuvus*, They are beating one another; *Si kamiu a vartapetape kamiu*, That ye love one another.

Reflective Verbs.

A reflex action is conveyed by the use of the adverb *kel*, 'back.' I strike myself: *Nau we vus kel nau*, " I strike back myself."—"He strangled himself," *Ni me ligo mate kelua*.

XI. REDUPLICATION.

Reduplication of substantives and verbs, adjectives and adverbs in a less degree, is very common and quite systematic in Mota.

Words are reduplicated in *three ways* :—

1. By the reduplication of the first consonant and vowel.

2. By the reduplication of the first close syllable.

3. By the reduplication of the whole word.

For example : *pute*, 'to sit,' — *pupute*, *putpute*, *putepute*.

The force of these reduplications is as follows :—

1. *Continuance*, prolongation of the act: *pupute*, ' keep on sitting.' The reduplicated syllable may be repeated as often as the idea requires.

2. *Intensification.*—The force of the word is magnified, the notion is more forcibly expressed: *putpute*, ' to sit closely down, to squat ; ' *siksike*, ' to seek earnestly.' This form of reduplication is that which most naturally applies to adjectives, substantives and adverbs : *manmantagai*, ' very small ; ' *Gate panpanei !* ' Oh, what hands ! what big hands ! ' *manmantag*, ' very well indeed.'*

Though the first close syllable is taken (a consonant being taken from the next syllable very often to close it as putpute, from pu te), yet when no consonant is at hand for the purpose, or only *r*, two syllables are taken, or made by adding e. Thus, *liwoa*, ' great,' *liwoliwoa ; purei*, ' unskilled,' *purepurei*.

3. *Repetition.*—The act done over and over again : *putepute*, to sit, get up, and sit again, and so on.

There are of course some words, as monosyllables, to which these rules do not exactly apply. In them, as indeed in all, the intonation of the voice does much to signify the notion conveyed to the reduplication.

XII. DIALECTS.

There are two dialects in Mota, with a few words of the vocabulary quite distinct, as *na* and *ge* for ' do,' *un* and *ima* for ' drink.' The difference chiefly lies in the preference for *u* in one, and *i* in the other, as *titin*, ' hot,' or *tutun*. The Veverau or leeward side of the island, use the *u*, and pronounce *g* at the end of word as

---

* This form of reduplication is continually used to signify number: *pispisui, rañrañoi*, 'fingers,' 'legs.' There are many words also which, probably for euphony, do not take any other form of reduplication than this : *ronronotag, valvalui*, ' hear ; ' ' answer.'

i,—*savrai* for *savrag*. They prefer *w* in many places to *g*, as *tawur* for *tagir*. In the termination of substantives the use of *i* or *u* is reversed in either dialect : *qatui* or *gatiu*, which in inflection gives *naqatuk, naqatuma* or *naqatik, tima*.

In the printed language, and in the form in which it is spoken by foreigners, the two dialects are now hopelessly confused. That of the leeward side, using *u*, is that which is best to follow,—at least in the main, as the best to connect with other dialects, and as giving more variety by the use of *u* and *i*, whether the other uses only *i*.

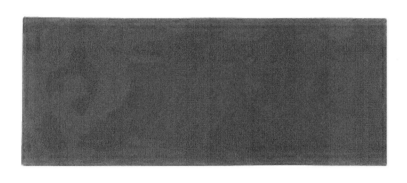

OPTIMIZING BINARY TREES GROWN
WITH A SORTING ALGORITHM

W. A. MARTIN -- D. N. NESS

421-69

OPTIMIZING BINARY TREES GROWN WITH A SORTING ALGORITHM

W. A. MARTIN -- D. N. NESS

Tree Growing Processes

In this paper we consider a process which grows and uses a labeled binary tree structure. Each node in this structure has an item of information, an upward pointer, and a downward pointer. The upward and downward pointers may point to null elements.

At any node in the strcuture all items of information in the *sub* tree *extending* which are larger* than the item of information at that node will be in the subtree pointed to by the upward pointer. Similarly, all smaller items are in the sub-tree pointed to by the downward pointer. In this paper we will not consider contexts where multiple nodes have the same item value.

Such trees are easy to grow. The first element is placed at the root. Thereafter each new element is placed in the tree by comparing it with the root and moving up or down depending on whether the new element is larger or smaller. This process is repeated at each node until an attempt is made to move to a null node. The item is then placed at this point in the tree. (We call this algorithm "A" below.)

---

*Obviously the measure can be any kind of computation.

As an example, consider adding the item 40 to the tree:

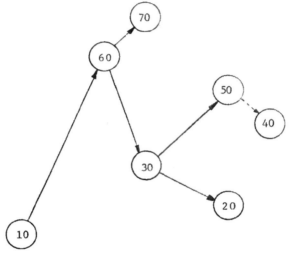

Figure 1

The following steps will be performed:

        1)   40 > 10 → move up

        2)   40 < 60 → move down

        3)   40 > 30 → move up

        4)   40 < 50 → move down

Since there is no item down from 50, 40 is attached at this point. This algorithm can be used for building symbol tables and it is closely related to the sorting algorithm, QUICKSORT (3,4).

Let us now consider some mathematical properties of the tree structures that are grown by this algorithm.

Mathematical Characteristics

The shape of a tree containing a given set of n items depends on the order in which the items are encountered by algorithm A. For example, the tree in Figure 1 was formed by considering the items in the order 10, 60, 30, 70, 20, 50, 40. By considering the same items in the order 40, 20, 60, 10, 30, 50, 70, the algorithm forms the tree in Figure 2.

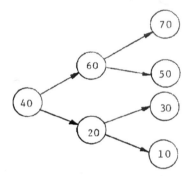

Figure 2

Algorithm A thus generates a tree for each of the n! possible arrangements of n items, but not all of these trees are distinct as can be seen from Figure 3.

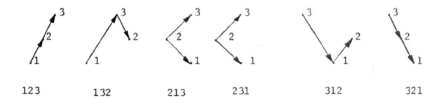

| 123 | 132 | 213 | 231 | 312 | 321 |

Figure 3

4

In the analysis to follow we will consider each of the n! permutations of the n items to be equally probable. Thus, some trees will be generated more often than others. We will also mention the results which obtain for the case where each distinct tree is taken as equally probable.

We can search for an item in a tree by following exactly the same steps used to insert the item while the tree is being constructed. It seems reasonable to assume that the time required is proportional to the number of nodes visited. (For example, see Figure 6) It is easy to see that one can find each of the items in the tree in Figure 2 by visiting a total of 17 (= 1*1 + 2*2 + 4*3) nodes, while one must visit 22 (= 1*1 + 1*2 + 2*3 + 2*4 + 1*5) nodes to find the same items in the tree in Figure 1. Clearly, the tree in Figure 2 is not only better, but optimum.[*] We have devised an algorithm (Algorithm B), presented below, which will convert any tree generated by Algorithm A into an optimum tree containing the same items. Algorithm B requires a time proportional to the number of items (see Figure 7). It is natural to ask whether the time thus saved in searching a reorganized tree is greater than the time required for the conversion from the non-optimal into the optimal form.

To this end, let us calculate the number $\bar{V}(n)$ of nodes visited per item, in finding each item in each of the n! trees containing n nodes. Let $V(n)$ be the number of nodes visited in finding each item in each of

---

[*]See Reference (5), page 402.

the n! trees with n nodes. The root node of each tree will be accessed n times; the total number of root node accesses summed over all trees is thus n·n!. Now, for $1 \leq k \leq n$ exactly n!/n trees have item k at the root node. If item k is at the root node there is a tree of k-1 items below the root node and a tree of n-k items above the root node. In the (n-1)! trees with item k at the root node, each of the (k-1)! trees containing k-1 items occurs (n-1)!/(k-1)! times below the root node. Similarly, each of the (n-k)! trees containing n-k items occurs (n-1)!/ (n-k)! times above the root node.

Therefore, we can write $V(n) = u(n, n!)$ where

$$u(n,m) = n \cdot m + 2 \sum_{k=0}^{n-1} u(k,m/n)$$

u(n,m) represents the number of node visits summed over all trees of n nodes, where the forest (collection of trees) consists of m trees. The formula can be obtained by observing the root node is visited n times for each tree in the forest, or a total of n·m node visits. For each value of the root node (1/n of the trees in the forest have the same root nodes) the upper (and lower) trees are a forest of m/n trees, and consist of k (k = 0, . . ., n-1) nodes. Thus the rest of the upper (or lower) tree requires $\sum_{k=0}^{n-1} u(k,m/n)$ visits.

Since $\overline{V}(n) = \dfrac{u(n,n!)}{n!}$

we want to find $\overline{u}(n,m) = \dfrac{u(n,m)}{m} = n + \dfrac{2}{n} \sum_{k=0}^{n-1} \dfrac{u(k,m/n)}{m/n}$.

2)*

---
*

6

So we can see by induction that $\bar{u}$ is not a function of m and we can

write $\quad \bar{V}(n) = n + \dfrac{2}{n} \sum\limits_{k=0}^{n-1} \bar{V}(k).$ \hfill 3)

From this we find

$$\bar{V}(n) = \frac{n+1}{n} \bar{V}(n-1) + 2 - \frac{1}{n} \hspace{2cm} 4)$$

and

$$\bar{V}(n) = - n + 2(n+1) \sum_{i=2}^{n+1} \frac{1}{i} \hspace{2cm} 5)*$$

The sum in 5) can be bounded by the log function to give the bounds.

$$\bar{V}(n) < - n + 2(n+1) \log n \hspace{2cm} 6)$$

$$\bar{V}(n) > - n + 2(n+1) \log \frac{n+1}{2}$$

Thus, for large n we have $\bar{V}(n) \simeq 2n\log n.$ \hfill 8)

This result has been obtained by Hibbard (3).

Now, for comparison, we derive an expression for the number r(n) of node visits for an optimum tree of n items. If $2^j - 1 \le n \le 2^{j+1} - 1$ we have

$$r(n) = \left(j2^j - 2^j + 1 \right) + (j + 1)(n - 2^j + 1) \hspace{2cm} 9)$$

In order to compare the average trees with the optimum, the function $\dfrac{\bar{V}(n) - r(n)}{r(n)}$ is plotted in Figure 5. For the plotted values the optimum tree gives an improvement of 10 to 30%. To examine this improvement

---

*Note: $\bar{V}(1) = 0$

$$\sum_{i}^{j} x^i = \frac{x^{j+1} - 1}{x - 1}$$

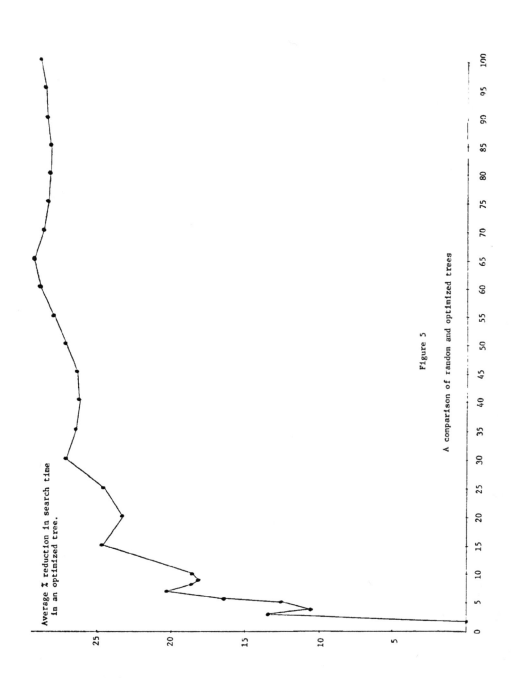

Figure 5

A comparison of random and optimized trees

further note that for large n and for $n=2^j-1$, $r(n)$ approaches $\dfrac{n \log(n)}{\log 2}$.

The improvement is then $\simeq$ .386 nlog n (.386 = 2 log 2 - 1).

Since the time it takes our Algorithm B to form an optimum tree is proportional to n, there is some n beyond which application of the algorithm must result (on the average) in a saving.

Referring to Knuth (5) we may also note that if we take all distinct labeled trees to be equally probable we obtain the result $\overline{V}(n) \simeq n\sqrt{n}$ for large n. This would make application of our algorithm even more profitable on the average. It suggests that those distinct labeled trees which are generated more than once by Algorithm A are often the "good" ones.

The above calculation suggests exactly how inefficient we can expect the "average" tree to be. It must be recognized, however, that the actual tree grown in any given case may depart even more substantially from the optimum. If the data were to be incorporated in ascending sequence, for example, each item would be placed "up" from all previous items, and our process would reduce to linear search with a time to access all items proportional to n^2.

It is obviously easy to extend the algorithm presented above to allow us to maintain information about the efficiency of the structure as it is being grown. If we start a counter at 1 and then increment it each time a comparison is performed in the process of placing that element in the tree, we obtain a count of the number of comparisons necessary to

find this element. If we accumulate this number as we bring in each new item we will always have the number of node visits to access all items availab

This information may suggest, then, that at some point it would be worth restructuring a tree as it is being grown or after it has been grown but before some searches are to be performed. We now present our algorithm for performing this restructuring.

The Restructuring Algorithm (Algorithm B)

The algorithm is presented here in English; it is also presented in the Appendix in FORTRAN.

The procedure IBEST returns as its answer a pointer to the root node of the restructured tree. This procedure also establishes the environment for the other subroutines: IGROW and NEXT. IBEST computes IGROW(n), where n is the number of nodes in the tree to be restructured. It returns the result of this computation (which is the restructured tree) as its answer.

The procedure IGROW(n) is responsible for constructing an optimum tree containing n nodes. It must be recursive as it may call itself. It uses the procedure NEXT, which returns a pointer to the smallest node in the old tree the first time it is called and a pointer to the smallest node not previously returned on each successive call. IGROW(n) can take three courses of action:

1) If n = 0 , return a pointer to a null node.

2) If n = 1 , call NEXT and return its result.

10

3) If n > 1

    a) Call IGROW ($\lfloor (n-1)/2 \rfloor$)

    b) Call NEXT

    c) Call IGROW ($\lceil (n-1)/2 \rceil$)

Then alter the node pointed to by the result of b) by replacing its up pointer with the result of a) and its down pointer with the result of c). Return the result of b), thus altered, as the answer.

The procedure NEXT moves through the original tree structure returning the nodes in ascending sequence. Given a tree, it returns the nodes in the lower branch by calling itself recursively with this branch as argument, then it returns the root node, and then the nodes in the upper branch. It is convenient to think of NEXT and IGROW as coroutines. It should be noted that IGROW does not need to modify the pointers of any node until NEXT is completely through with it. Thus the nodes of the original tree can be patched directly and no additional memory is required.

Incremental Restructuring

If one wishes to form an optimum tree each time a new node is added, then it is not necessary to use a global restructuring method like Algorith B. A method which concentrates on those nodes visited during the addition of the new node can be used. We are not aware of such a method which is highly efficient. However, a good method is known for maintaining a tree structure which may not be optimum, but is very good (1,2).

11

This tree structure is characterized by the constraint that the maximum path length of the subtree above a given node cannot differ by more than one from the maximum path length of the subtree below that node. This constraint excludes the really bad trees formed by algorithm A and so the average number of nodes visited per item searched must be less than 2logn, but slightly more than for an optimum binary tree. This has been verified numerically by Foster (2). Such a tree is shown in Figure 4.

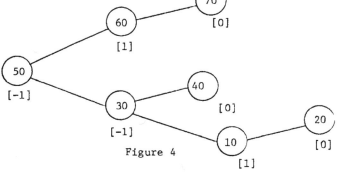

Figure 4

In order to make the method of adding a new node efficient, each node must have associated with it a number indicating the amount by which the maximum path length of the upper subtree exceeds the maximum path length of the lower subtree. In Figure 4 these numbers are shown in brackets next to each node. A new node is added to this structure in two steps. First, the node is added to the tree using algorithm A. However, a pointer to each node visited should be placed on a push-down-list so that the path can later be retraced to restructure the tree. (Note that

the tree cannot be altered to meet the path length constraint until
the new node is in place, because the maximum path length of a subtree containing the new node depends on exactly where the new node
is added.) The tree is then restructured by applying algorithm C. To apply this algorithm one traces back along the path
followed in adding the new node. At each node along this path one
of the following conditions will hold:

    a. Either the upper or lower subtree was previously longer by
       one and now they are the same length. In this case no re-
       structuring is needed and it is not necessary to move back
       toward the root node any farther since the length of the
       subtree extending from this node is unchanged.

    b. Both subtrees were previously the same length and now one
       of them is longer by one. No restructuring is done but the
       path must be retraced farther, since the length of the sub-
       tree extending from this node has increased by one.

    c. A subtree which was previously longer by one is now longer
       by two. The tree must be restructured at this node but the
       path need not be retraced any farther since the restructuring
       will return the subtree to its original length.

    In order to explain the restructuring algorithm let us assume that
the lower subtree is longer, so that the tree has the form.

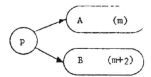

13

A and B are subtrees of length m and m+2 respectively. To restructure we save a pointer to node p and examine subtree B. It will either have the form:

I)

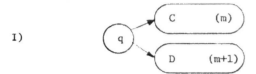

or the form:

II)

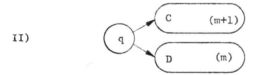

since it was of length m+1 before the new node was added, and the new node increased its length without unbalancing it so that it needed to be restructured.

In case I) the restructuring is completed by forming the tree:

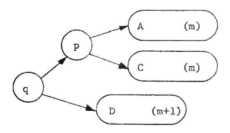

14

In case II) we examine subtree C. If $m \neq 0$ it will have one of the forms:

III)

IV) For $m = 0$ subtree C will just be a single node.

In case III) the restructuring is completed by forming the tree:

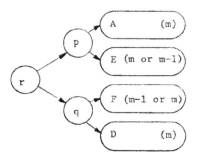

Finally, in case IV) the final tree has the form:

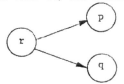

One can now verify that each of these restructuring operations returns the subtree to its length before the new node was added. Furthermore, it is easy to see that the effort required to restructure once a node with unbalanced subtrees has been located is independent of the size of the entire tree.

15

No one has given an exact analysis of the effort required to add a new node to the tree and then retrace the path until a node in either condition a) or c) is found. Foster (2) argues that for large trees the average effort to retrace and the fractional number of times each case of restructuring is applied are independent of the size of the tree. If this is the case then the total average effort to apply algorithm C while building a large tree is proportioned to n, the number of nodes, just as it is for algorithm B.

A Comparison of the Global and Incremental Restructuring Algorithms

We can then propose two strategies for building a tree of n items.

a. Apply algorithm A n times and then apply algorithm B once.

b. Apply algorithm A n times and apply algorithm C each time algorithm A is used.

Strategy a) will require an effort $A_1 n \log n + Bn$, for some constants A_1 and B. Strategy b) will require, under the assumptions of Foster, effort $A_2 n \log n + Cn$. Strategy b) keeps the tree organized at each step and this would tend to make A_2 less than A_1. On the other hand, strategy b) requires saving pointers to the nodes visited on a push-down-list and this would tend to make A_2 greater than A_1. Strategy a) always leaves us with an optimum tree while strategy b) leaves us with a tree which is slightly less than optimum. In addition, strategy b) requires slightly more storage.

16

Experimental Results

Programs for strategy a) and strategy b) were coded in FORTRAN for the IBM 1130. Algorithm C is longer and more difficult to program than algorithm B. Figure 6 shows the average compution time/ node visited as a function of the size of the tree being searched by algorithm A. Trees of a given size were generated at random; the same results also held for worst trees.

Figure 7 shows the average computation time/item for application of algorithm B to random trees of different sizes.

Figure 8 shows the average time/item to apply strategy a) and strategy b) as a function of the size of the tree. The solid line is fitted to the points for strategy a) and the broken line is fitted to the points for strategy b). It can be seen that strategy b) is slightly faster for trees of less than 1000 items.

Conclusions

Trees grown without any reorganization are quite good on the average. Reorganization is a second order improvement, and so a decision to use algorithm B or algorithm C depends on how the information is to be accessed.

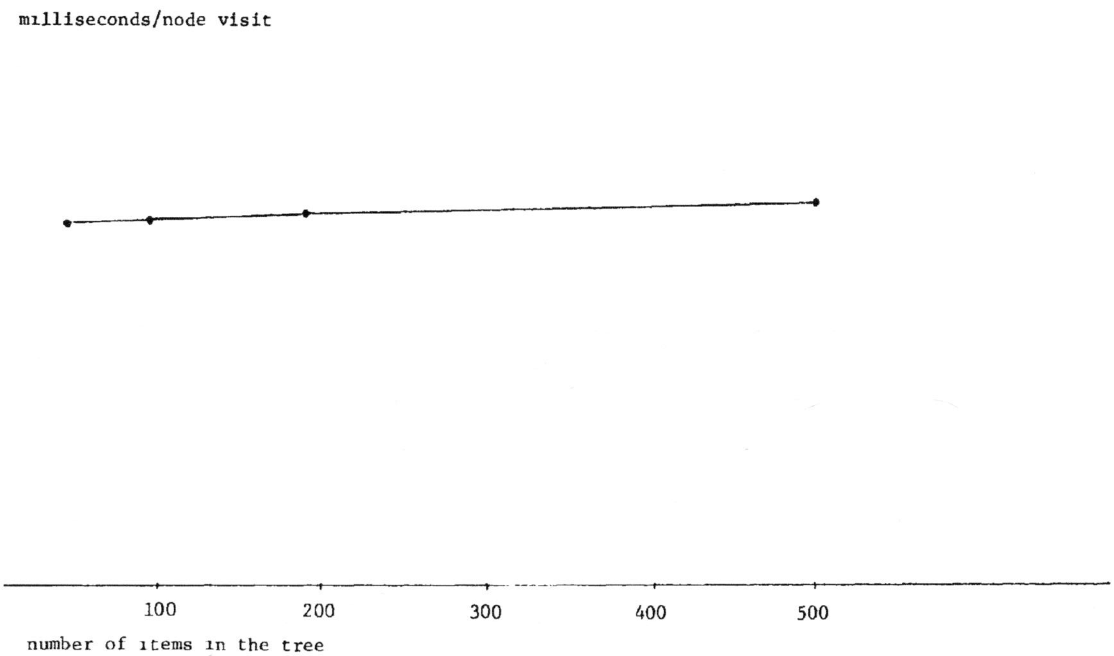

milliseconds/node visit

number of items in the tree

100   200   300   400   500

Figure 6

The time required for algorithm A to visit one node
for random trees of different sizes. (The shape of
the tree does not change the time within the accuracy
of this graph.)

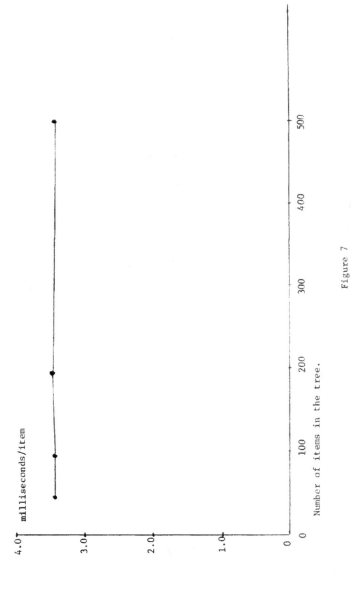

18

Figure 7

The time required to apply algorithm B.
(The shape of the tree does not change
the time within the accuracy of this graph.)

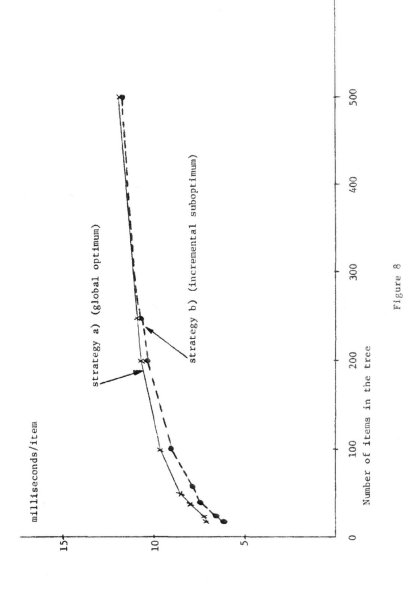

Figure 8

The time/item to grow and optimize a tree.

```
C      **************************************************************
C      ********** ALGORITHM A                                    ****
C      **************************************************************
C      DATA ITEMS IN 'ITEMS'
C      UPWARD POINTERS IN 'IUP'
C      DOWNWARD POINTERS IN 'IDOWN'
C      PUSH-DOWN LIST FOR NEXT IS NPDL, INDEX IS NPDLI
C      PUSH-DOWN LIST FOR GROW IS MPDL, INDEX IS MPDLI
C      CURRENT NUMBER OF ITEMS IN 'IN'
C      BEGINNING OF TREE IN 'IBEG'
C      IUP, IDOWN, ITEMS, NPDL AND MPDL MUST BE DIMENSIONED
C      INITIALIZATION
       IN=0
       IBEG=1
C      ...
C      PUT AWAY THE ITEM IN 'ITEM'
       IN=IN+1
       ITEMS(IN)=ITEM
       IUP(IN)=0
       IDOWN(IN)=0
C      IF IT IS FIRST ITEM IN LIST, RETURN (VIA STATEMENT 30)
       IF(IN-1)100,30,100
C      NOT FIRST ITEM IN LIST, PLACE IT
  100  ICUR=IBEG
  110  IF(ITEMS(ICUR)-ITEM) 120,120,150
C      GOES IN UPWARD TREE
  120  IF(IUP(ICUR)) 140,130,140
C      PLACE IF UPWARD TREE EMPTY
  130  IUP(ICUR)=IN
       GO TO 30
C      UP ANOTHER BRANCH
  140  ICUR=IUP(ICUR)
       GO TO 110
C      GOES IN DOWNWARD TREE
  150  IF(IDOWN(ICUR)) 170,160,170
C      PLACE IN DOWNWARD TREE
  160  IDOWN(ICUR)=IN
       GO TO 30
C      DOWN ANOTHER BRANCH
  170  ICUR=IDOWN(ICUR)
       GO TO 110
C      RETURN TO PROGRAM
   30  ...
```

```
C     ***************************************************************
C     ********** ALGORITHM B                                 ********
C     ***************************************************************
C     INITIALIZATION
      NPDLI=0
      MPDLI=0
      NPDLU=IBEG
C     CALL IGROW(IN)
      IG=IN
      IGR=1
      GO TO 800
 240  IBEG=IANS
C     'IBEG' NOW POINTS TO BEGINNING OF RESTRUCTURED TREE
C     RETURN TO MAIN COMPUTATION
      . . .
C     ***************************************************************
C     ********** SUBROUTINE IGROW                            ********
C     ***************************************************************
C     ARGUMENT IN 'IG'
C     RETURN VIA 'IGN'
C     ANSWER TO 'IANS'
 800  IANS=0
      IF(IG-1) 830,810,840
C     IGROW(1), RETURN INEXT
 810  INR=1
      GO TO 900
 820  IUP(IANS)=0
      IDOWN(IANS)=0
C     GENERAL EXIT
 830  GO TO (240,850,870),IGR
C     IGROW(IG), IG 1, PUSH DOWN AND CALL
 840  IGN=(IG-1)/2
C     SAVE RETURN AND NUMBER TO CALL WITH NEXT TIME
      MPDLI=MPDLI+2
      MPDL(MPDLI-1)=IGR
      MPDL(MPDLI)=IG-1-IGN
C     CALL IGROW(IG) RECURSIVELY
      IG=IGN
      IGR=2
      GO TO 800
C     RETURN FROM RECURSIVE CALL, CALL NEXT
 850  IG=MPDL(MPDLI)
      MPDL(MPDLI)=IANS
```

```
          INR=2
          GO TO 900
C         RETURN FROM NEXT, CALL IGRCW RECURSIVELY AGAIN
  860     MPCLI=MPCLI+1
          MPCL(MPCLI)=IANS
          IGR=3
          GC TC 8CO
C         RESTRUCTURE AS IS APPROPRIATE
  870     IG=MPCL(MPCLI)
          IUP(IG)=IANS
          IDOWN(IC)=MPCL(MPDLI-1)
          IANS=IG
C         POP THE STACK AND RETURN
          IGR=MPDL(MPDLI-2)
          MPCLI=MPDLI-3
          GO TO 830
C         ************************************************************
C         ********** SUBROUTINE NEXT                           *******
C         ************************************************************
C         NPCLU CONTAINS NODE TO BEGIN DOWNWARD PATH, UNLESS ZERO
  900     IF(NPDLU) 910,920,910
C         PUSH CURRENT NODE AND CHAIN DOWNWARDS
  910     NPDLI=NPDLI+1
          NPDL(NPDLI)=NPDLU
          NPCLU=IDOWN(NPDLU)
          GO TO 900
C         NO FURTHER CHAIN, RETURN A VALUE AND POP STACK
  920     IANS=NPDL(NPDLI)
          NPDLI=NPDLI-1
          NPCLU=IUP(IANS)
C         EXIT
          GO TO (820,860),INR
          END
```

REFERENCES

1. Adel'son-Vel'skiy, G. M., and Landis, Ye. M., "An Algorithm for the Organization of Information," Deklady Akademii Nauk USSR, Moscow, p. 263-266; Vol. 16, No. 2, 1962; also available in translation as U.S. Dept. of Commerce OTS, JPRS 17,137, Washington, D.C., and as NASA Document N63-11777.

2. Foster, C. C., "Information Storage and Retrieval Using AVL Trees," Proc. ACM 20th National Conference, (1965), p. 192-205.

3. Hibbard, T. N., "Some Combinatorial Properties of Certain Trees With Applications to Searching and Sorting," JACM 6 (May 1963), 206-213.

4. Hoare, C. A. R., "Algorithms 63, Partition, and 64, Quicksort," CACM 4 (July 1961), p. 321.

5. Knuth, D. E., The Art of Computer Programming, Vol. 1, Addison-Wesley, (1968), Section 2.3.4.5.